Kathleen Lee Dong

SURVIVING SILENCE

How to cope with and overcome silent treatment

Mindscribe Press

2023

Definition of Silent Treatment

"Silent treatment" (also known as "wall of silence") is a passive-aggressive behavior in which a person, instead of communicating openly and addressing a conflict or issue in a relationship, deliberately chooses to ignore the other party or refuse to interact verbally or emotionally with them. This behavior may manifest itself through complete silence, avoidance, emotional detachment, and failure to respond to messages, phone calls, or requests for communication.

Silent treatment can have a significant impact on relationship dynamics, causing tension, emotional stress, and damage to communication. Often, those who use silent treatment do so with the intention of controlling or manipulating the other person, trying to gain control or to punish them for some reason. It is important to note that this behavior can be detrimental to the relationship and requires proper management to be addressed and overcome in a healthy way.

The Power of Silence

In the course of human relationships, we encounter a wide range of challenges and conflicts. Some of these challenges are met with open dialogue and always seeking constructive communication, while others, unfortunately, come up against the impenetrable wall of silence chosen by others. This chapter will explore in detail the "treatment of silence" and the inevitable power it wields in relational dynamics.

Emotional Effects

Anyone who has ever experienced silent treatment knows how emotionally devastating it can be. It is as if the ground beneath our feet collapses, leaving us at the mercy of emotions ranging from confusion to anger, from sadness to anxiety. The feeling of being ignored or excluded can make us feel insignificant and unwanted, shaking our self-esteem and causing an unbearable sense of isolation.

Psychological Effects

In addition to the immediate emotional effects, silent treatment can inflict lasting psychological damage. Persistent failure to communicate and respond to our requests can undermine our confidence in ourselves and in the person who is giving us silent treatment. Prolonged silence can give rise to a state of chronic stress and even lead us to depression, as our mind is constantly struggling to understand the conflict and its resolution.

The Dynamics of Control

One of the most insidious features of silent treatment is its power to exert a form of control within relationships. Those who use silent treatment generally try to manipulate the situation, forcing the other party to seek his favor or forgiveness. In this way, those who decide on silent treatment can feel in a position of power, while those who undergo it feel powerless and at the mercy of others' decisions.

Unilateral Communication

Another troubling aspect of silent treatment is its tendency to create one-sided communication. In these situations, one party dominates the conversation, or rather non-conversation, imposing its own point of view without listening to or considering the needs of the other. This imbalance in communication can have lasting negative effects on relationship dynamics, undermining mutual trust and understanding.

The Long-Term Consequences

The consequences of silent treatment are not limited to the present. Often the emotional wounds caused by prolonged periods of silence can persist even after reconciliation. Relationships can suffer irreversible damage, and the effect of silent treatment can reverberate over the long term, hindering personal growth and the relationship itself.

Before delving into strategies for coping with and overcoming silent treatment, it is important to consider the actual value of silence as a tool for conflict resolution or for expressing our different needs as human beings. A specific and critical analysis of silent treatment will help us better understand why it can be so damaging to relationships and prepare us for the path to healing and eventual reconciliation.

The Emotional Impact of Silent Treatment

In human relationships, communication is the key to mutual understanding, conflict resolution and the building of deep bonds. However, the emotional impact of silent treatment can cause cycles of isolation and disconnection within relationships, whether these are between couples, friends, or even between parents and children.

The Force of Silence
Silent treatment is an act of active denial of communication, in which a person deliberately chooses to ignore the other party or refuse to respond verbally or emotionally. This behavior can manifest itself through complete silence, avoidance and emotional detachment. The

emotional impact of silent treatment is often devastating for the sufferer.

Emotions Unleashed

Anyone who has experienced silent treatment knows how distressing it can be. The emotions that emerge in this context vary, but can include anxiety, frustration, sadness, anger, and confusion. The feeling of being ignored or excluded makes the affected person feel as if they have no voice or value in the relationship. These emotions can trigger a range of reactions, from desperate attempts to re-establish communication to painful introspection about one's self-worth.

Psychological Damage

In addition to the immediate emotional effects, silent treatment can inflict lasting psychological damage. Persistent lack of communication and unresponsiveness to requests can undermine confidence in oneself and the person giving silent treatment. Prolonged silence can lead to a state of chronic stress, fueling constant thinking about what went wrong and why communication failed. As we have already mentioned, one must be very careful, because this situation can even result in symptoms of depression and psychiatric problems.

One of the most insidious dynamics associated with silent treatment is its ability to exert control within relationships. Those who use it often do so with the intention of manipulating the situation, forcing the other party to seek his or her favor or forgiveness. In this way, the giver of silent treatment can feel in a position of power, while the sufferer feels helpless like a puppet in the hands of a puppet master.

Because silent treatment creates one-sided communication, in which one party dominates the conversation, imposing its own point of view without listening to or considering the needs of the other, a harmful imbalance in communication is created precisely because the person giving silent treatment seeks to control the narrative and make the other party feel guilty or at fault.

This is why silent treatment can trigger cycles of isolation and disconnection within relationships. The person affected by silent treatment often tries to re-establish communication at any cost, but this quest can be fruitless and only lead to further emotional pain. Over time, these continued negative interactions can erode the bond between those involved and create a downward spiral of disconnection and resentment.

We need to be clear that the emotional impact of silent treatment is always significant and damaging to relationships, and those who choose it often do so consciously precisely to destroy or drive away the other person. Understanding the power of silence is the first step toward managing and resolving this destructive behavior. In healthy relationships, open communication and mutual respect are essential. Dealing with silent treatment requires honest dialogue and a desire not so much to rebuild the bridge of communication, but to take an introspective journey within oneself to free oneself from this destructive dynamic.

Why do people use silent treatment?

People may use silent treatment for various reasons, which may include emotional, psychological, and relational aspects. It is important to note that silent treatment is almost always a passive-aggressive behavior, and the reasons why it is used may vary from individual to individual. In any case, let us try to list some of the most common reasons behind the use of this punitive attitude:

Control and Handling
Some people use silent treatment as a means of exerting control over others. By ignoring the other party or refusing to communicate, they try to make the other person feel guilty or helpless, pushing them to do what they want.

Punishment

Silent treatment can be used as punishment for alleged unwanted behavior or to express disagreement. Those who use it hope that the other person will feel guilty or repentant about what they have done or said.

Escape from Conflict

Some people use silent treatment to avoid confrontation or debate about a problem or conflict. Instead of confronting the situation openly, they prefer to ignore it and hope it will resolve itself.

Need for Space

In some cases, silent treatment may be a response to a need for personal space or time to reflect. However, it is important to distinguish between the legitimate need for space and the harmful use of silence to manipulate others.

Reaction to Emotional Wounds
Those who use silent treatment might do so as a reaction to emotional wounds or hurt feelings. These people emotionally isolate themselves as a defense mechanism to avoid further injury.

Lack of Communication Skills
Some people may use silent treatment because they do not know how to express their feelings or needs appropriately. Silence becomes an easy alternative to open communication.

Narcissism or Egocentrism
In some situations, silent treatment may be linked to narcissism or self-centeredness. Those who use silent treatment may do so to feed their ego or to draw attention to themselves.

Learned Cycles of Behavior

Those who grew up in an environment where silent treatment was a common way of handling conflict might repeat this pattern of behavior in adult relationships.

It is important to note that in many cases these motivations overlap. It is important to make an honest analysis of the other person's personality to understand why we have been subjected to this treatment and whether we should leave the field before it is too late. In healthy relationships, on the other hand, it is essential to look for more constructive ways to manage conflict and communicate one's needs.

The different faces of Silent Treatment

Silent treatment in the couple

Silent treatment within a couple is almost always passive-aggressive behavior.
The reasons why it is applied can be:

1. Repressed Frustration:
Silent treatment may result from the difficulty of expressing one's frustration or anger in an open and constructive way. A partner may prefer silence to avoid saying things he or she feels are hurtful or harmful.

2. Fear of Conflict:
Some people try to avoid direct confrontation for fear of making the situation worse or hurting

their partner's feelings. Instead of confronting the problem, they use silence as a way out.

3. Need for Control:
Silent treatment can be a way to exert control within the relationship. Those who use it try to make the other partner feel guilty or get what they want through emotional detachment.

4. Unresolved Emotional Wounds:
This behavior may be a reaction to emotional wounds or unresolved past events. A partner might use silence as a form of punishment or to brood over previous situations.

Consequences of Silent Treatment in the Couple

1. Emotional Distance:
Silent treatment creates an emotional barrier between partners, causing increasing distance and alienation.

2. Insulation:
Those experiencing silent treatment may feel isolated, helpless and unwanted in the relationship. This can lead to feelings of loneliness and depression.

3. Resentment:
The silent treatment partner may build up resentment and anger, which further undermines the relationship and creates a vicious cycle of conflict.

4. Lack of Communication:
Lack of open communication prevents conflict resolution and mutual understanding, hindering the couple's growth.

5. Destructive Cycle:
Silent treatment can create a destructive cycle in which the behavior is repeated and intensified over time, severely undermining the stability of the relationship.

Thus, we are talking about a serious impediment to communication and emotional connection. Addressing this behavior requires a thorough analysis of the underlying causes and a commitment from both partners to restore communication and mutual respect in the relationship.

Silent treatment among friends

The treatment of silence between friends shares some similarities with what happens in couple relationships, but there are also some important differences due to the nature of different relationships.

In a couple relationship, in fact, there is often a high degree of intimacy and emotional dependence between the partners. In friendship relationships, on the other hand, emotional dependence can vary greatly. While some friends may be very close and share many aspects of their lives, others may maintain a greater emotional distance. As a result, the emotional impact of silent treatment may vary depending on the degree of intimacy between the friends involved.

The motivations behind silent treatment may be similar in both couple relationships and between friends, such as fear of conflict or the need for control. However, silent treatment between friends could also be due to specific friendship-related issues, such as a disagreement on a particular topic or situation. In addition, it may occur because of some change that occurred in the friendship group dynamic or social events that triggered the reaction.

The consequences of silent treatment between friends may vary depending on the strength of the friendship and the ability to deal with the conflict. In some cases, silent treatment may even lead to the rupture of the friendship, especially if the behavior is repeated or not addressed constructively. However, in more solid friendships, the people involved may be more inclined to resolve the problem and restore communication.

When silent treatment involves an entire group of friends rather than just two people, it can affect the overall group dynamic. For example, a friend who decides to ignore another group member can cause tension and division within the group. This can lead to complex situations in which other friends must mediate or take sides.

It is also true, however, that in the context of friendships, the restoration of communication may be more flexible than in couple relationships. Friends can reconnect more easily, unless the silent treatment has led to deep emotional wounds or irreparable damage. However, even between friends, addressing the problem and addressing the underlying causes remains essential to resolving the situation.

Silent treatment in the family

Silent treatment within the family can have particularly complex dynamics and consequences, given that these are bonds that are often more enduring and deeper than friendships or couple relationships.

Within a family, ties are much more deeply rooted and profound than in other relationships. There are ties of kinship and shared history that can make silent treatment even more painful and emotionally burden it with more unresolved questions. Family members know each other intimately, which can lead to a deeper understanding of relationship dynamics, but it is equally true that silent treatment in the family can be triggered by a wide range of causes, including quarrels over inheritance issues, divisions of responsibility or decisions regarding the family, among others. In addition, sibling competition or rivalry dynamics may emerge that contribute to this form of manipulation or punishment.

Certainly, silent treatment can have significant consequences on the family unit: it can lead to a breakdown in communication and increasing distance between family members. In some situations, silent treatment can even lead to the ultimate breakdown of ties.

When silent treatment involves the parents or primary janitors of the family, it can have a particularly significant impact on children or adolescents. They may feel confused, anxious and traumatized by the lack of communication and family tensions.

Sometimes, other family members, such as brothers, sisters, or extended relatives, may try to act as intermediaries to try to resolve the situation or try to bring the conflicting family members together. But this can be complicated and requires a lot of patience.

What's more, if silent treatment was a role model used by parents or older family members, younger people might learn this dynamic and replicate it in their future family or personal relationships.

In some cases, therefore, silent treatment in the family may require the intervention of a counselor or family therapist to help members understand the root causes of the behavior and develop strategies to restore communication and family cohesion.

Silent treatment at work

This is a phenomenon that can also have a significant impact on the work climate and dynamics between coworkers or between supervisors and employees.

The work context is different from personal relationships because it is centered on business goals, organizational hierarchies, and professional responsibilities. Silent treatment in the workplace can have a direct impact on employee productivity, cooperation, and morale.

Causes of silent treatment in the office can vary and may include conflicts over work issues, rivalry between colleagues, misunderstandings or personal quarrels that are reflected in the work environment. In some cases, silent treatment may be used as a passive-aggressive tactic to gain an advantage or to manipulate a situation. It is the employer's responsibility to pay attention to the existence of these dynamics within his company, and if he is the first to implement them, he should soon question the reasons why and try to work to improve his communication skills.

When team members or colleagues stop communicating openly, it can indeed be difficult to solve problems, exchange crucial information, or work together to achieve common goals.

The use of silent treatment can negatively affect employee morale and the work climate. Individuals undergoing silent treatment may feel isolated and stressed, which can damage their emotional well-being and affect their motivation.

Therefore, business organizations must promote a culture of open communication and constructive conflict management. Silent treatment goes against these principles and may require the intervention of human resource managers or superiors to try to resolve the situation and restore communication between the parties involved.

In addition, silent treatment between a supervisor and an employee can be particularly problematic because the supervisor has a direct influence on the employee's career and professional growth. This type of behavior can generate a tense work environment and undermine trust between the employee and the employer.

Using the weapon of silence can certainly pose a risk to the organization as it can contribute to the creation of tensions and destructive conflicts. In addition, it can lead to the isolation of an individual within the organization, possibly affecting his or her job performance and satisfaction.

In conclusion, silent treatment in the workplace is a behavior that can have significant consequences on the work climate, communication, and collaboration among employees. Companies and workplaces should promote a culture of open communication and provide means to address and resolve conflicts constructively in order to maintain a healthy and productive work environment.

How to recognize silent treatment

Recognizing silent treatment is critical to addressing the problem and trying to solve it. Although those who experience it know exactly what it is, I list some unmistakable signs that can help you identify silent treatment within different types of relationships.

Communication Disrupted: One of the most obvious signs of silent treatment is the complete breakdown of communication by a person. This may include refusal to respond to calls, texts, e-mails or requests for verbal interaction.

Emotional Detachment: The silent treatment user may show obvious emotional detachment. He may seem cold, indifferent, or even hostile, whereas in the past he was more open or affectionate.

Avoidance of Conversations: The person who is implementing silent treatment toward you may try to avoid situations in which it would be necessary to communicate with you or address the problem. For example, he or she may leave the house or stay in another room during a discussion.

Refusal to Resolve Problems: People who use silent treatment tend to refuse to discuss or resolve problems or conflicts. He or she may ignore your requests for clarification or even attempts at discussion.

Prolonged Silence: Silent treatment is not just a brief period of silence after an argument. It is prolonged behavior in which a person refuses to communicate for an extended period, often without any apparent justification.

Changes in Behaviors: Silence may be accompanied by changes in behavior. The person may avoid participating in shared activities, such as going out together or attending social events.

Exclusion: The silent treatment giver may try to exclude the target person from social circles or shared activities. He or she may act as if the other person is no longer a part of his or her life.

Emotional Manipulation: Silent treatment can be used as a form of emotional manipulation to make the other person feel guilty or to get what is desired.

Changes in Relational Atmosphere: The use of silent treatment makes the atmosphere within the relationship tense and stressful. One may feel that something is wrong, but one does not know what.

Emotional Reactions: The silent treatment sufferer may react with anxiety, frustration, sadness or anger. He or she may feel confused or hurt.

Therefore, you must always remember that silent treatment is passive-aggressive behavior. If you recognize these signs in a relationship, it is important to deal with the problem constructively or move away from this personality type early.

To understand when to run away and when to make an attempt at reconciliation, it is necessary to make a fundamental distinction.

Differences between silent treatment and the need for space

"Silent treatment" and the need for space are two very different concepts, although both can result in a period of reduced communication within a relationship. Recognizing these differences is essential to avoid misunderstandings and conflict in relationships. Silent treatment can be harmful and counterproductive, while needing space can be a healthy way to manage tensions or intense emotions.

Here are the main differences between the two:

Silent Treatment

Rationale: Silent treatment is generally passive-aggressive behavior that is intended to punish or manipulate the other person. The giver of silent treatment may be angry or hurt and uses silence as a weapon to make the other person feel guilty.

Communication Blocked: Communication is deliberately blocked by one of the parties, who refuses to respond or interact with the other person. There is no openness for problem solving or discussion.

Duration: Tends to be prolonged in time, sometimes for days or weeks, and may persist until the person using it achieves his or her emotional goals, such as feeling apologetic or getting what he or she wants.

Negative Consequences: It usually has negative consequences on the relationship, causing emotional distance, resentment and tension.

Need for Space

Rationale: The need for space is often motivated by personal needs for reflection, recovery, or stress management. It is not intended as an act of punishment or manipulation toward the other person.

Open Communication: Communication remains open, but the person may ask for some time and space for himself or herself. She is willing to discuss her needs with the other person.

Limited Duration: It is usually temporary and time-limited. The person asks for time to deal with a situation or set of emotions, but does not make a sustained commitment to silence.

Beneficial to Relationship: Unlike silent treatment, the need for space can be beneficial to the relationship in that it allows the people involved to manage their emotions in a healthy way and then return to open communication and problem solving.

In summary, the main difference between silent treatment and need for space is the motivation behind the behavior and the nature of the communication. While silent treatment is harmful behavior intended to punish or manipulate, need for space is a legitimate request for time and space to deal with personal emotions or stressful situations, and should be respected.

The Roots of the Problem

We anticipated that the underlying causes of silent treatment may vary from person to person and situation to situation. However, there are some common causes that may contribute to this harmful behavior.

One of the most common causes is pent-up anger or frustration that has not been expressed appropriately. A person may build up resentment and choose silence as a means of avoiding saying things that he or she feels are hurtful or harmful.

Indeed, some people avoid confrontation at all costs for fear of making the situation worse or hurting their partner's feelings. Silent treatment thus becomes a way to escape uncomfortable discussions or open conflict.

Silent treatment can also be used as a way to exert control within the relationship: the user tries to make the other partner feel guilty or to get what he or she wants through emotional detachment.

Unresolved emotional wounds or past events that may be an underlying cause states of silent treatment should also never be underestimated. The person may use silence as a form of punishment or to brood over previous situations.

In some cases, we said, silent treatment may result from a lack of communication skills. The person may not know how to express his feelings or needs appropriately and uses silence as an easy alternative. This is an easier case to deal with because one can try to get the other person to think about the need to follow a path in which he or she can learn to communicate in a healthy and trusting way, unfortunately, however, in some situations, silent treatment may result from a lack of empathy for the other person. The person may not be willing to consider the feelings or needs of the other partner. This is the case when this treatment is linked to narcissism or self-centeredness. The person who uses it might also do it to feed his or her ego or to draw attention to himself or herself.

People who have had past experiences of abandonment or betrayal may be more likely to use silent treatment as a self-defense mechanism to avoid further emotional wounds. And unfortunately, this is the most common case they face.

Narcissism and silent treatment

Narcissism and silent treatment are two psychological phenomena that can intertwine in complex and harmful ways.

Narcissism is a personality trait characterized by excessive self-love, a need for admiration and a lack of empathy for others. People with narcissistic tendencies may have a high sense of self-worth, but this may hide an underlying emotional fragility. Narcissism can exist in various forms and degrees, from healthy to pathological narcissism.

The link between narcissism and silent treatment can be complex but significant because people with narcissistic tendencies may seek to exert dominant control within relationships. Silent treatment can then become a tool to gain this control, making the other person feel anxious or guilty.

Although they appear to have high self-esteem, people with narcissism are very sensitive to criticism or perceptions of abandonment, so silent treatment may be a reaction to narcissistic offense as the person tries to protect his or her ego.

Narcissism, then, is often associated with a lack of empathy toward others. Those who use silent treatment may not consider the harmful effects of their behavior on the other person because they are unable to put themselves in the other person's shoes.

Since the narcissist is accustomed to emotional manipulation, silent treatment can also be-it almost always is-an underhand way of manipulating the situation. The user may expect the other person to make efforts and beg him or her to get close again, thus satisfying the narcissistic need for adoration and attention. But it is a satisfaction that is almost always short-lived. In fact, the narcissist is not really interested in the other person, and likewise the purpose of his silence may be precisely to get rid of the other person, someone he no longer cares about. To do so by silence is to get him off his back without accounting for why and without taking his pain into consideration.

When narcissism and silent treatment become intertwined, they can thus create a destructive cycle within the relationship. The other person may feel increasingly isolated and hurt, while the silent treatment user may become increasingly demanding and incapable of satisfaction.

Relationships characterized by narcissism and silent treatment can be extremely difficult to manage. It is essential to recognize harmful behaviors in order to get out of this mechanism as soon as possible.

Communication problems

Communication is the connective tissue of human relationships. It is through communication that we express our thoughts, share feelings, solve problems and build meaningful connections with others. However, when communication becomes faulty or lacks altogether, problems that undermine the health of relationships are inevitable.

Silent treatment is in its own way a form of communication, but it is a distorted form of communication in which one person deliberately chooses not to communicate with another. Clearly, this can be devastating for the person undergoing it, because it represents a refusal to enter into dialogue and address problems together. We have already mentioned that the causes of silent treatment can vary, but they are often related to underlying communication problems.

These problems are often serious and can manifest in many forms. One of the main ones is the lack of active listening.

When we do not listen carefully to what the other person is saying, we not only miss the opportunity to understand them, but also to make them feel valid and seen. Active listening, on the contrary, involves paying complete attention to what is being said by the other person, asking questions to clarify and trying to put ourselves in the other person's shoes.

Empathy is a key element of effective communication, because only through empathy are we able to understand and share the feelings of others. When empathy is lacking, communication becomes cold and disengaged.

Open communication is also crucial, especially in resolving conflicts constructively. This means creating a space where both parties feel free to express their thoughts and feelings without fear of judgment or criticism. Open communication requires the courage to face uncomfortable discussions, but it is essential to maintaining a healthy relationship.

However, it is important to avoid criticism and blaming during the conversation, because silent treatment is often a reaction to criticism or accusation. Avoiding criticizing or blaming the other person can help maintain a constructive tone and avoid the use of silent treatment in the future.

Acknowledging differences is also important: people have different perspectives, experiences, and feelings; seeing and respecting these differences is critical to effective communication. Instead of trying to convince the other person to think or feel a certain way, you can try to understand their perspectives.

Addressing communication problems takes time and commitment. Often, it can be helpful to learn communication skills through therapy or counseling. These professionals can teach strategies to improve communication and deal with conflict, because communication, I will never tire of repeating, is the cornerstone of healthy relationships.

People deal with conflict differently depending on their personality, past experiences, and acquired communication skills. Some people are inclined to avoid conflict at all costs, fearing that it will damage the relationship or lead to further tension. In contrast, other people may be more inclined to seek open confrontation, hoping to resolve the situation soon. For example, if one person is inclined to avoid conflicts and the other prefers to confront them openly, a situation may arise in which one person chooses silent treatment as a way to avoid direct confrontation.

It is important to recognize these differences and try to work together to develop a conflict management strategy that works for both. It can take time, mutual understanding and, in some cases, the involvement of a counselor or therapist to help mediate differences and teach coping strategies.

Trying to understand the other person's point of view, even if it is different from your own, can help prevent destructive conflicts and help build a stronger and healthier relationship in the long run.

The Silent Treatment Cycle

How the cycle develops

The silent treatment cycle is a pattern of behavior that can repeat within a relationship even several times when one of the partners uses this form of punishment or manipulation. This cycle can vary in duration and intensity, but usually always follows a similar pattern. Here is how it develops:

1. The Accumulated Voltage:
The cycle of silent treatment always begins by using accumulated tension within the relationship as fuel. This tension may arise from disagreements, misunderstandings, or unresolved problems. At this stage, emotions

such as irritation, frustration, and anger may rise.

It is important to note that the accumulated tension is not communicated openly, but accumulates below the surface, often due to lack of communication.

At this stage, emotions such as irritation, frustration, anger and disappointment may rise. Lack of confrontation and open discussion can cause these feelings to increase, further fueling tension.

2. The Beginning of Silent Treatment:
When tension reaches a critical point, one of the people involved in the conflict may decide to initiate silent treatment. This behavior may be motivated by a desire to punish the other person or difficulty in managing one's emotions. The person using silent treatment withdraws

emotionally and decides to stop communicating with the other person.

We have seen how this behavior can be motivated by a variety of factors: the person using silent treatment may perceive that the other person deserves punishment for something he or she has done or said, his or her intent is thus to make the other person feel guilty or repentant, or he or she may want to avoid confrontation and open discussion at all costs. Silent treatment may thus be a way to avoid addressing an uncomfortable topic or to avoid having to admit that he or she is wrong.

Those who use silent treatment may find it difficult to express their emotions in a healthy and assertive way. Silence becomes a way of protecting oneself from intense or conflicting emotions.3.The Silent Period:During this phase, silence prevails The person who initiated the silent treatment avoids all forms of communication with the other, ignoring calls, texts and requests for interaction. This silent period can vary in length, from hours to days or even weeks.

The duration often depends on the severity of the conflict and the determination of the person using silent treatment. Communication is completely disrupted.

4. The Growth of Emotional Detachment:

During the silent period, emotional detachment between the people involved increases. This is often one of the most damaging consequences of the cycle, as emotional detachment can cause deep damage to relationships. Those experiencing silent treatment may feel increasingly isolated and confused, while those using it may feel justified in their behavior (this phase can lead to a feeling of power or control).

One may perceive that silence is a means to get what one wants or to make the other person feel guilty.

5. Reapproach Attempts:

At this stage, the silent treatment sufferer may make attempts to reconnect and reopen communication. These attempts may include apologies, pleas, or promises of change. However, these requests often fall on deaf ears or are ignored.
This can further increase the frustration and confusion of the person trying to reconcile.

6. Reapplication or Cycle Repetition:
In some cases, the cycle of silent treatment may end with a temporary reconciliation, in which the people involved return to communication. However, if the underlying causes of conflict are

not addressed and resolved, the cycle is likely to repeat itself in the future, creating a damaging dynamic within the relationship.

Repeated cycles undermine the couple's trust, communication, and stability. To break this cycle, it is critical to address the underlying problems in an open and constructive manner. It takes time, mutual understanding and, in some cases, the involvement of a counselor or therapist to help mediate the situation and develop healthier strategies for dealing with conflict.

Coping with Silent Treatment

Confronting silent treatment in a healthy way can be a challenge, but it is essential to preserve the health of relationships and promote open communication. There is no other way to do this than to start by confronting yourself and repeating the steps that need to be followed.

My advice is to take a sheet of paper, write the titles of these steps as a decalogue and hang it in a place where it can be seen as often as possible.

1. Recognize Your Feelings:

First of all, it is important to acknowledge your feelings. You may feel frustrated, confused, angry or hurt. These feelings are legitimate and valid. Take the time to examine your emotions and understand how you are feeling.

2. Keep Calm:

Avoid responding to silent treatment with anger or revenge. Keep calm and control your emotional reactions. The silent treatment may be an attempt to get a reaction from you, so reacting emotionally can further fuel the negative dynamic.

3. Communicating Openly:

When you feel ready, try to communicate openly with the person using silent treatment. Be kind and respectful, and try to create an environment where you can both talk freely. Express your desire to resolve the conflict and restore communication.

4. Avoiding Blame:

When talking to the person using silent treatment, avoid blaming them or directly accusing them of their behavior. Instead, share your feelings and experiences objectively. For example, you can say, "I feel confused and worried when you stop talking to me."

5. Listening Actively:
Listen carefully to what the other person has to say if he or she decides to open up. Try to understand his or her perspectives and feelings. Active listening is key to establishing a connection and better understanding the situation.

6. Seek Support from a Therapist:
If silent treatment persists or if the situation is particularly difficult, you might consider involving a therapist or counselor. A mental health professional can help mediate the situation.

7. Learning to Manage Conflicts:
Work on your ability to handle conflict constructively. This includes learning assertive communication strategies, managing emotions during a discussion, and seeking solutions to problems together.

8. Establishing Healthy Boundaries:
If silent treatment becomes a pattern of harmful behavior in the relationship, consider setting healthy boundaries. Set clear expectations about communicating and dealing with conflict constructively. If the person continues to use silent treatment persistently, you may have to make more drastic decisions to protect your emotional health.

Remember that dealing with silent treatment requires patience and time. It will not always be possible to solve the problem immediately, but working on open communication and mutual understanding can help improve the situation in the long run.

Certainly dealing with punitive silence can be a difficult and frustrating situation. But your self-reflection is necessary to honestly assess whether there have been situations of conflict or tension in your recent interactions such as to lead to this attitude. This can help you better understand the situation and demand the respect you deserve. Remember that you can always ask the other person why he or she is silent.

If the other person continues with the "silent treatment," respect his or her need for space. Forcing communication could make the situation worse. Therefore, give the person time to reflect and find ways to deal with the issue.

Even if you feel anger or disappointment, when the person is ready to communicate, practice active listening. Listen carefully without interruptions, judgments or emotional reactions and try to understand his or her perspectives and concerns.

Also avoid responding to the "silent treatment" with more silence or counterattack. Maintain a respectful tone and try to keep communication open.

If the situation is not resolved, consider involving a mediator or a couples or relationship counselor. These figures can help facilitate more constructive communication and find solutions.

The most important thing however is to take care of yourself because silence can be emotionally devastating. Make sure you take care of your emotional health. Seek support from friends, family or a mental health professional if you feel you need it.

Remember that although it may be difficult, you cannot control the actions of others. You can only manage your own response to the situation. The important thing is to try to remain calm, promote open communication, and respect the other person's boundaries.

How to avoid negative emotional reactions

Avoiding negative emotional reactions when faced with silent treatment or confrontational situations is a difficult challenge, but it can be tried through awareness and practice.

The first step in avoiding negative emotional reactions is to become aware of your emotions. Before reacting, ask yourself, "How do I feel right now?" Acknowledging your emotions is key to managing them in a healthy way. You may feel angry, hurt, frustrated, or sad, and all of these emotions are legitimate.

When you feel that negative emotions are taking over, take a pause and breathe deeply. This simple act can help you relax and regain your composure. Take a moment for yourself if necessary. There is no need to immediately respond "to the affront" of silence....

It is always best to avoid confronting silent treatment or conflict situations while you are still emotionally charged. An emotional confrontation can intensify conflict and lead to impulsive reactions. Wait until you feel calmer and more focused.

When you decide to address the problem, focus your attention on communication rather than emotional reaction. Express your feelings objectively and respectfully, avoiding the use of accusatory or hurtful words. Focus on what you want to communicate and how to improve the situation.

Active listening is a key skill to avoid negative emotional reactions. When the other person speaks, be fully present and try to understand his or her perspectives and feelings. This shows respect and opens the door to mutual understanding.

Often, silent treatment or conflicts have underlying causes. Try to find out what might be at the root of the problem. We have listed many of the reasons that can lead to this behavior and by now you should have an idea. There may be worries, fears, or unmet needs that contribute to this behavior. Recognizing these causes can help you find more effective solutions.

Emotional education is crucial to avoid negative emotional reactions. If you think you don't have the skills, learn to manage stress through techniques such as meditation, yoga or exercise. These practices can help you stay calm even in difficult situations.

If you find it difficult to avoid negative emotional reactions such as anger and despair on your own, consider involving a counselor or therapist. These professionals can teach you skills for managing emotions and dealing with conflict.

It is not always easy, but it can be done. Take the time to acknowledge your emotions, breathe deeply, focus on constructive communication and try to understand the other person's perspective. With time and practice, you will be able to handle conflict situations in a calmer and more positive way.

Here is a little reminder of how you can at least try to keep your cool in the most difficult situations.

Emotional awareness is the first step in learning to manage emotions. Take time to examine your emotions, recognize them and accept them without judgment. Ask yourself what you are feeling and why. This will help you understand yourself better.

Remember that deep breathing is a quick and effective way to calm the nervous system. When you feel your emotions intensify, take a few deep breaths, inhaling slowly through your nose and exhaling through your mouth. This can help you regain calmness.

If you have never done so, consider meditation-a great way to learn how to manage your emotions. Mindfulness meditation teaches you to be present in the present moment and to accept your emotions without judgment. It can help you develop greater emotional resilience in these circumstances. You don't need to take complex courses; sometimes small visualization techniques are enough.

Positive visualization for example is a technique that allows you to imagine situations in which you react in a calm and assertive way. Practice visualization of yourself dealing with silent treatment or other conflicts in a calm and controlled way. You will see that you will understand a lot about yourself.

Above all, since emotions can be intense, it is sometimes helpful to find constructive ways to vent them. You might consider exercise, journal writing, painting, or practicing hobbies that relax you.

Emotions are a response to our interpretations of situations. Ask yourself what thoughts or beliefs might be fueling your emotions. Recognizing these causes can help you manage your emotions more effectively.

Be patient with yourself as you develop these skills. Don't expect to be perfect, but try to improve gradually. A healthy lifestyle, with good nutrition, adequate sleep and exercise, can help maintain a stable emotional balance.

Keeping calm and learning to manage emotions requires constant practice, but these skills can have a significant impact on your ability to deal with conflict situations constructively and maintain healthier relationships.

Overcoming Silent Treatment

Scientific research on the psychology of relationships has revealed several reasons why people may use this tactic-we all know them by now.

But even though it seems extremely hard, overcoming silent treatment and rebuilding communication requires a joint effort by both people involved in the relationship. Both people must engage in open and empathic communication. This means actively listening to each other, without judgment, and trying to understand each other's perspectives and feelings.

Set clear expectations about communication and how to deal with conflicts in your relationship. This can help prevent the recurrence of silent treatment.

If you have already tried to communicate and have not gotten a response or positive change, you can set a time limit. Tell the person that if you cannot establish open communication within a certain period, it will be necessary for you to move on.

Most importantly, keep your commitment: if the deadline expires and the situation does not improve, keep your decision to move forward. It may be difficult, but it is important for your emotional health to avoid such a damaging dynamic. It is no longer important why the person is behaving this way. What matters now is you.

Talk to friends or family about what you are facing. Find in them emotional support. If you are in too much pain, turn to a professional to help you process your feelings and experiences. In case you don't have the right financial support to do so, you can read additional books about it, such as "Nonviolent Communication: A Language of Life" by Marshall B. Rosenberg.

In short, focus your attention on yourself. Take time to heal, to discover new activities or hobbies, and to build healthier and more constructive relationships with other people.

Remember that making the decision to say goodbye to someone who uses "silent treatment" is a personal choice, and should be made for your emotional well-being.

The Silence is broken.

Now, you are ready to look forward.

Silence can be frightening, but it no longer has power over you. You have learned to recognize it, defend yourself and seek communication .

Remember, forgiveness does not mean forgetting or justifying the harmful behavior, but rather freeing oneself from its grip and moving forward with one's head held high.

Surviving "silent treatment" is only the beginning. Protecting your emotional health is critical to building healthy and mature relationships. Establish healthy boundaries, communicate openly and honestly, and maintain your inner calm even when silence threatens to engulf you. Your emotional health is a precious treasure; guard it carefully.

The time has certainly come for healthy and fulfilling relationships; it is possible even if you don't see them on the horizon now. You can apply your skills to build stronger, more mature relationships. Remember that relationships take work, but your commitment and understanding can make all the difference.

I invite you to live without silence. There is no more room for "silent treatment" in your life.

*The Reality of The Other Person Lies Not In What He Reveals To You, But What He Cannot Reveal To You.
Therefore, If You Would Understand Him, Listen Not To What He Says, But Rather To What He Does Not Say.*

Khalil Gibran

If this book has been helpful to you, please consider leaving a review on Amazon. Your review will contribute to its wider reach and impact, making it a valuable resource for others.

KATHLEEN LEE DONG

GRAY ROCK

THE SECRET METHOD TO CHANGE YOUR INTERACTIONS WITH NARCISSISTS AND MAKE THEM HARMLESS

CLIMBING NARCISSUS

PATHOLOGICAL NARCISSISM IN WORK AND CAREER. HOW TO MANAGE YOUR BOSS AND COLLEAGUES

Kathleen Lee Dong

KATHLEEN LEE DONG

How to respond to a narcissist
in all situations

Mindscribe Press

Kathleen Lee Dong

SELECTIVE

EMPATHY

MINDSCRIBE
PRESS

THE INVISIBLE TRAUMA

growing up with a narcissistic
father or mother

KATHLEEN LEE DONG

KATHLEEN LEE DONG

YOU KILLED ME

Why do men continue to kill women?

MINDSCRIBE

Printed in Dunstable, United Kingdom